involutia

Other works of poetry by Deborah Meadows include:

Thin Gloves (Green Integer, 2006)
Growing Still (Tinfish Press, 2005)
Representing Absence (Green Integer, 2004)
Itinerant Men (Krupskaya Press, 2004)
"*The 60's and 70's:* from *The Theory of Subjectivity in Moby-Dick*"
(Tinfish Press, 2003)

Deborah Meadows

involutia

Shearsman Books
Exeter

First published in in the United Kingdom in 2007 by
Shearsman Books Ltd
58 Velwell Road
Exeter EX4 4LD

www.shearsman.com

ISBN-13 978-1-905700-19-6

ISBN-10 1-905700-19-9

Acknowledgements
'Logic with Mr. Quine' appeared as a *WinteRed* chaplet. 'Animated
States' first appeared in *The Poker*, and is forthcoming in *The PIP (Project
for Innovative Poetry) Anthology*, Volume 8 (Los Angeles: Green Integer).
Other poems have appeared in *Antennae, Tinfish, Fence, Fourteen Hills* and
Shearsman. The author would like to thank the editors of these literary
publications.

Cover:
Ordos belt plaque, bronze
Buffalo Museum of Science
catalog number Br66
photographer: KC Kratt

The publisher gratefully acknowledges financial assistance for its 2005-2007
publishing programme from Arts Council England.

Contents

for Howard

Part of a rich tradition of poetry and commentary, *Secrets of the Blue Cliff Record* contains some of the most known and least known koans. Luce Irigaray and Gilles Deleuze have accidental meetings as "Luce" and "Gilles" at study.

Luce Studies the Blue Cliff Record

Haven't I?

Haven't I said that?

Haven't I made enough?

So if she is restrained from images
        except through him, we have a problem
        of subjectivity
But her body could be other than his version
        A defensible space for
        creation of things
A name not closer to nature as a sensual flow
        but evocative exploration of sexual fusion
Accomplished by woman & man
        without dividing roles.
Does not adhere to grid, follows
        heat of the moment
Not clearly laid out or articulated.

                          *

At high noon, there's no need to point east
        or define west anymore.
Yet conditions persist, how to take pulse of ailing
        or relieve pain?
        Did you walk all over with those
dirty shoes on?
                Turning your back
on interpretation as if literatures were
the size of a thumbnail
falling into type?

    . . . A time that follows heat
of the moment, beyond particulars,
      names, and distinctions.

      Giving oneself to be shaped
in a manner she cannot predict
      To enhance the porous nature
of the body—moment to moment
      Made an act mutual with time,
a membrane of pleasure
      Pursuit of what cannot be represented,
but why the philosopher's task
      of regenerating whole cultures?

           *

This is why closing and opening
      are equally taught.
Perception joined to application
      (holding still)
      temporary is true: expert shows
      her moves to a weak opponent
              Be sure not to glance aside
at new plants with weak roots.

As a condition that makes it
can break it: unrepresented yet constitutive.
        Can read the texts for bias & subordination,
discover a new subject
lurking in the wings.
        Not premised on lack, she unsettles
contemporary structures of language.
        Without overlooking theatrical space-time,
its props & dialogs, steep recess into distance,
its splayed forefronting of intimacy or action,
        she said, "specular economy."
                To speak of thresholds & fluids,
shape of eroticism rather than scoping
detached parts, pliable
"landscapes."
                So risking confusion, we must.

                        *

The philosopher, to say it in everyday terms, came to the edge
of the stagnant water of transcendence.

To cut through interpretations before the mirror
        loses its light.

The whole scene reveals your culture, its
        sound and form—an absorption in frolic.

without neglecting characteristic fluids
without neglecting characteristics of property
without neglecting characteristics
                              that are tactile
              that are difficult to idealize
              that are difficult to make stable
              that are difficult to resist

Here, rubbings between two infinitely near
              neighbors
              stirrings between two infinitely near
              neighbors
              blendings between two infinitely near
              neighbors

There, a break between perceptible & intelligible,
              a break between mounting a scale of value,
              a break between "nature" put onto nature

                              ★

If you have eyes, look!

If you have hands, touch!

This is no more mystic . . .
than words *straight to the point*,
clear as pond water.

when she takes
when she takes up
when she takes up his work
reworking the question of language "on trial"
    from the philosophical tradition.
She is writing *with* him;
she says, he is a partner in a love
            relationship.
Not his double, she wants him to hear her call
    from beyond
    the circle of his work.

Why would she reflect another detached image
        to him, reiterate "same" to
        confirm his illusion of self?

                    ★

Stuck in conventional truth is imagining
        radiant light will emerge from a stump.

He hangs out a sheep skin,
        but sells dog meat.

The stink of religion
        coating everything.

sensual forms through which perception
                              manifests,
no over-emphasis on sight

there is a space between phallic gods &
        the rest of the world

she may cover & dwell in all things

        how closed is the word from everything?
how happy when both reflect, and so make the other?
        or not all, but a small, small angle.

                    *

Without dwelling on anything, four gates.

Go on through, standing erect like
the free birds we are.

A flow, a percolation,
a favored edge.

            when he is forgetful of *she* who gave birth to him,
a protégé is born
            from a sea
            of becomings
is the "he" pronoun,
"I" prosthesis
            at false center of false pattern
linking events by corrosive illusion
            without exalted matter,
            we-they-you-she
                        at passages

                        *

A monk shouts, then hits another
so radiant light is emitted
from bugs, dirt, and worms

"no guts" & "high opinion of himself"

he would like to use her
"while remaining safe in port"

. . . in material existence, there's self-consciousness
          even by mere mention

she shares lips and her edges
          her coral involutions
          trimmed

                              some opaque matter
                              makes possible
                                        variation

not made
with words

                    *

with finger-pressed crumbs
great teachers cannot be paid

great oaks are not crumbs
but scenes, the path
          of language ends later

but for the pretense
of crumbs and oaks, well,
that's another matter!

slip, slip, slipped from the picture

       inherent properties
       (spliced with language

had we looked keenly
toward theatre conventions
          to penetrate Western thought
its geometries,
      overview, its slow dissolve?

what word describes a *"what* without properties
necessary for conventions with properties"?

             ★

whiskers of an ant

one pound of feathers, weigh it yourself!

blinded by clichés, enter an *empty* valley.
     When will you ever get out?

. . . refusal, not hate.

She, a stranger in her own land,
had never threatened "system" with exposure
to its hidden non-events
        nor had she refined disorder.
                A smooth narrative,
it said of itself,
pocked with events
that culminate in culmination.

                    ★

When rain falls on the lake,
it's hard to distinguish edges.
        But the lake
        is not the whole world.

One substance so recondite
        even a needle for silk
        can't penetrate.

vitality of material
                    elements as they flow together
                    and fall apart
kaleidoscopic pattern
were it by sound

            projecting into the other, receiving
from the other—steep drop in tone,
pick-up sticks
that old time rhythm

                            *

The hermit spent that winter
reducing all wisdom to
        all aggregates are impermanent

Unclimbed, sharp defile,
perch in battle

no opening for comparison.

when I opened my eyes,
I was no longer in contact
with the rest of the world . . .

when I opened my eyes,
I was part of the perceptual flow . . .

when I opened my eyes,
all was significant yet shifting . . .

when I opened my eyes,
I never felt as awake . . .

when I opened my eyes,
a shimmer in ordinary leaves
laid over the world . . .

*

seeing mountains,
seeing how mountains are seen,
seeing mountains

reducing mother to substrate
            of father-son
as multiplicity without
        a face,
or taking away her
        creativity
the provision his blind spot makes
            makes to foreclosed chance
        at other ways

other ways, out of same-and-same,
a cord to Wholeness

                    *

what one uplifts, another suppresses

Who is breaking out or in? Where
        are the weeds?

        The adept tires at sitting.

   language mis-ruled by old logic
may be an example
   flesh-made-word not impeded
by divisions
   a feeling of fire against Pure reason
makes public that speech how

   things thrown in steep shadow
or against its camera angle

   am-are, was-were retain being
or absence of being
   How habits of the body render one.

*

Teachers propose what doesn't exist
at moments they may be honored.
Philosophers propose what doesn't exist
making monuments, turn
centripetally toward seamless earth

first, second
veils, passages

sucking-substitutes might
                    carry
                    messages
touch so it's felt inside, not merely
on the surface. See, all begin with
differing aptitudes for pleasure. But
can be educated from there, typical.

That makes the rules
hides the source.
                              Carnal breathing
exercises,
            body I give back to myself.
                              Training inner to
outer, a "-ness."

                    ⋆

The president asked, "What is known about
            our past?"
The philosopher had no conclusion;
The poet said, "Embodied as words,
            a seal reproduces."

set to the mind regarding, between us
love *to* you, I give it

listening
                        through
                                    as grow you deeply

having taken away
this and that, we're down to it
            a bump, an incipient
                        uncracked stone
            of Thou.

                                    *

This corner suggests three more.

Three more are neither emerging
            nor not-emerging
                        outside of pattern.

How to compare this with before the flower blossoms?

Gilles Studies the Blue Cliff Record

I have experienced the "arrival scene"
as if it were my own.

I have fallen-in-love as a cultural
trope with all its features.

I have perpetuated inequality without
awareness or disturbance of everyday life.

I have recognized backlit heroic
stances as objective reportage.

*

Making a gesture of fright: cane
    thrown down, a way
    of handling the snake.

Obliterate tracks, standing as a state.

Look at your feet as *expedient* means,
    look to the figure within a word
      as figurative, by rate.

parts inside others, the way

we distinguish them from other things
presupposes stratified societies that select
                        certain
                        connections
                        over
                        others
What of other syntheses? connections?
                dynamic flows? fluid feelings?
                (propulsions that can also dissipate)

                        *

Diamonds are tested with glass
        Zennists with a single word.

How are tests tested then?

The better grindstone
wears down dull edges.

Go where no one can spy,
        but how is everywhere made even more?

between the lines
        mouth speaking in dialog
        with points

going from one to the other
        source & commentary

stitched through, abundance
        of radiant lines
        until no more thread can fit
        in original hole. Not the point.

                *

If position is removed from potential,
play of emerging-and-subsiding.

        The foliage is splendid indeed,
        the capital city still far away.

Of ashes ahead

So in my name
or through multiplicities that traverse me,
        converse with me,
        posit me,
        fluctuate me.

Spread from margin to perimeter,
        voluptuous machine of a zone
                more recondite for its language
than intention.

                *

In teachings, sown & collected
        are not the same. No more
clay funerary figure, skillful resemblance.

Two players know all in's-and-out's
of one another's game, unreadable
from the outside.

        A philosopher conceives new knives.
First perception, then language.
        Tree of completion, empirical dragon.

        double negation
        he is not that he is
        reactionary nomad

subjectivity as outcome   implications
        happens to fall
        from his own perspective
        to excessive birth of genre
and synthetic trope.

                    ⋆

        I'm not a great teacher either
                I've already told you too much.

        Is it something descended from heaven
                (a precious sword?)
        Is it something that welled up from earth
                (an element that gives or takes?)

        myriad forms & dimensions
                the little cup afloat
                raises a wave.

Sources include: works by Irigaray, by Deleuze, *Secrets of the Blue Cliff Record* (Thomas Cleary, translator), and *Irigaray and Deleuze: Experiments in Visceral Philosophy* by Tasmin Lorraine.

Animated States

Uncertain on structure's relation anymore
to containment or plenum, an eligible

subject mounts with time making accrual
a force less set-like than a hard summons

of injustice defined in the immediacy of a crowd's cry.
Long, slow, subtle remedy washes over incompletion

even adding more fractured dispersal to old-time stories;
parsed by theme, comparativists roll out by rack,

the tree, its "up" side read as text, not agency
of circulation, a soul's voyage on tired road

uphill giving weight to mortal objects cast aside
conditioned by such context as two-fifths pain

makes the man to legalistic cohorts so rational
to administer and *fair*, as legible as waves,

though consider for a moment difficulties fraught
with decline and you have an explosive situation

on your hands, tilted track beyond switch-yards
and right-of-way conflagration fed by sparked

weeds, though ahead of myself here, analysis runs
from naturalized narrative and back until change

inhabits structure ghosting the screen moderates
claim they can bring to crisp clarity, adjustments,

moving furniture, re-seating the seated, who,
once again, managed to lose entrusted with it all

down to spent round establish optimism.

Midnight in Our Motivated

Right here, an alternate reading or despair our conditions?
Suggestion of foul play makes us experimental partners tentative

in keeping beat as nationalist pulse that races,
arranged in steps. But then coming down, erratic

words in mold and stale bread, informational or distilled
story, no unturned example, unpermitted dumping

altogether-now when most attacked historically –
At reading, our meter for conditioned signs now bypassed,

valid signature, worked valve, slick-faced
interference, rolled up welcome mats, suspicion –

now that's another story: hopped up percussionists
hum of air tankers on return circuit 'til it's out

emphasizing old taints and favors, impediments
liked for charting counterintuitive voting patterns

believers are no longer pulled inward to its great
or sundown, whichever comes first. A new science,

a sort of confusion using bad foot to drag good
as two ends reach across states' suspension.

Hadn't you hoped for a change adding fire,
telling-knots addressed to mind by hand, but the music

acquired measure runs its blood circuit, what's there
after midnight in our motivated glacial moraine. None.

No software adequate to discern delusion, an error
behind favoring the favored, never happens

yet how little we know of the world's composition
in just societies even in legislative form

or social constraint, those forces holding power of refusal
to natural domination, ill-gotten releases.

Products from agricultural regions compete for last:
feathers drop after double barrier, world becomes wide.

Irresistible volume to pattern desire, define equally
as mystify, knowing deferral works well –

boulder and drag-marks behind the car's embankment.
          The means already upon us completes
our education by vanishing, tools stuck with range:

limits embellish mortal compass with blurred sides, so true

*

Logic with Mr. Quine

Logic with Mr. Quine

The barber slips out to another village
                    for a shave, and so
                    for a time
is not a barber from that other village.

Still, no conclusion on
whether in the second village
                    he shaves himself or
                    is shaved by a second barber.

*

You can rely on it that
all poets are unreliable.

I am unreliable.

I am unreliable$_0$ when unreliable$_1$
            is appended to its own quotation, so
                    "yields an unreliable$_0$ result
                    when appended to its own quotation."

*

Truths that don't consist of provability.

Cold truths invest
        treatment for color schemes
roasted restaurant
        belonging to its self-set.

Drenched with ideas on type.

Membership seeming to disallow:

        not all the way in, or not
so clear.

He's someone who works
there, is known for it.
                Imagine how many poets
want something from him
they could actually enumerate
        Gawain trials
deep city thickets & noirish fog
        freeway embankments
come up
        leering questions
                differ from
        haunting questions

the way a breach of taste
magnifies force of money.

                *

Necessary Truths

1).

If little of our goings-on
go on
by necessity,
                    then little need for a word like

necessarily.

It ain't prescriptively so.

People go on:
Went on, much went on by necessity.

2).

If nearly all our goings-on
go on
by necessity,
              then little need for a word like

necessarily.

It goes without saying.

3).

Passing events are sorted
                            not sorted

by features of necessity.

          Will it also make me sick?
(not necessarily)
          Surely he will miss me
          when I'm gone?
(necessarily, bound to)

4).

When more sure than sure,
    no need for "surely."

If about to be shown a leopard,
    "surely it has spots"
        is predicted, so
out it comes
at leash-end

        governing the conditional sentence.

Note: (Suggested by W. V. Quine's *The Ways of Paradox and Other Essays*, p. 68)

I would like to ask the professor to discuss *iterative hierarchy* (begin with some non-sets, then form all possible sets of these, then form all possible sets of the things formed so far, then form all possible sets of these, and so on.) that Mr. Quine discusses. Somehow I suspect it will help me understand serial poems, their compositional principles better than I do now.

W. V. Quine, in his *The Ways of Paradox and Other Essays* writes: "This iterative picture of sets built up in stages contrasts with the older notion of the extension of a concept; these are sometimes called the mathematical and logical notions of collection, respectively. The early controversy over the paradoxes and the axiom of choice can be traced to the lack of a clear distinction between these at the time."

Carnap and Logical Truth

1).

If alternate systems of logic exist,
          then they would use "or"
"none" and "and" differently.

                    Prediction.

Natural languages translate
          one to another
from shared logic or not?

2).

To indicate membership overtakes
many other marks
invented, or at least used
for convenience
      in well-known ways.

Oh, my featherless biped.

      An abundance of framing
devices for empty sets.

3).

This sentence comes from
                    "this sentence"
            in a limited
            sort of way.

Do you use it differently?

Can we inject "equals" with content

beyond function?

4-6).

Not merely syntactical truths
    (matter of degree
              of indeterminacy
              of frequency, alternation

4).

Unconstrued, but elementary shapes
and elevations
                        departures from point
to the status
            or approach
to a course in water's properties.

5).

Elsewhere in the corpus
        purposes can enter.

Lawfully looked on
        our branches
        extend
material
and
set-like.

*

Someday I will ask W. V. Quine whether the relation a sequence has to infinity is strictly necessary.

Someday I will ask W. V. Quine whether the relation infinity has to sequence is necessary in the strictest sense.

Pets

1.

The sacred icons: Jackie's gloves, auctioned
document, curated iris

    more sacred than these this spring . . .

from debased work conditions, we turn to love
    can my skin your skin
        touch
    without ideology of valentine
without spectacles
        of the kind our kin bear?

How I like our "mere appearances."

2.

"The individual who in the service of the spectacle is placed in stardom's spotlight is in fact the opposite of an individual . . . In entering the spectacle as a model to be identified with, he renounces all autonomy in order himself to identify with the general law of obedience to the course of things . . . And Kennedy the orator survived himself, so to speak, and even delivered his own funeral oration, in the sense that Theodore Sorenson still wrote speeches for Kennedy's successor in the very style that had done so much to create the dead man's persona."

from Guy Debord's *Society of the Spectacle*

3.

Creating the dead's persona

(the absolute becomes historical)

as ever present power turns to close the door against winter
        and all our surroundings surround us
                in their contingencies

                gen: many one and one and one
                        depend from
                        penned from
                rendered pretty
                so pretty, we're blind
                        but now eye sea
                general forms
                in particular
                                stances,
                that's got his own

                        ★ ★ ★

                              discipline
or performance in the sentence
break when it completes
the action,

                              fills it with wet sand,
an iron ring next
to provide a shape

Singular as a pear
            threshold, a death
deflected by weight, gentle
as drop

                    * * *

handle
in complement,
neck in advance

* * *

Spin animal tales horn
experienced chiffon, the red horse
          Mercury cut into lobes
and trivial decoration

hesitations

* * *

★ ★ ★

exposed, found wanting, ultimately dismissed

ghost in the machine

what was so much there
just yesterday

bison underdrawing
in our discovered
cave

could work in
as movement

hide patterns

visual equivalent of an accent

★ ★ ★

* * *

Indefinite survival, somehow, fractures
the pivot pin, makes obsolete the arrow,
finds the code
                              a proper ration
cut to inform us.

Measured yet innocent, a mere example.
Corrupt-as or pure-as isometric
depiction, these fisheries.

                              Where an inch equals
sea trench, how difficult
to prevent the steep fall
from model to ideal.

* * *

★ ★ ★

that convene necessity or

The sort of appreciation a visual pun
evokes illustrating essentials of arranged
objects, where we learn it, what more
we can learn, our capacity
for topics whether mechanical, ideational,
violent, sound. Deployed as still life,
a domestic genre, we can import
popular things, soup cans and Marilyn,
replace a pear or moist rabbit with public things,
flatten surface to label,
linger over irreverence, note visual disappearance:
intentional and unintentional holds they have,
underneath and behind the urge for scatter.

* * *

Why performance can't shed instance
and gives it out breaking principles
of identity. Deep trust in bodily call
to rhythm, unsweetening the concocted breach.
Wind back these wild inferences,
this option, this time when we run out
of regular language. Recurrence that is not
the same defeats the argument of math
it loves most.

* * *

*

         excellence
to live in
to die in
your name comes up
         like your number
on a list, *The Iliad*

fame prolongs
     helps you adjust
     to battlefield
     conditions on a list
and poetry colludes

beauty colludes

*

I have cracked the code.

I have one again.

. . .

*

catalogues

Iliadic warriors

Whitmanic men and women.

*

*

Islands.

To carve vitality of cells.

Find us here inserted among a world of things.

Deduce from its "item" nature conclusions
        about our life there.

Parallel or clustered, as a mental activity, doubt
        and veracity based on bodily tests: what
        we can make out, what recedes to blur.

Having wanted expert results, had we over-desired
        the possible, curving space, light toward our range?

The length of it as lovely as its depth.

Here a nest, there a stage as subsets
        of Place where action conspires
        imperfectly with language.

Spoken as a conceit,
        how to re-fit colonial buildings for people.

*

Short Song, a portrait

Dreamed World

A dream quotes a world
   parted by this world's reduction.
      It spends but doesn't conserve.

Little darling replicant structure
      inhabiting me, everyone wants in
but only you reduce me.

     Saved pennies in a child's jar
emplots a trial run at tragic
      movement, curling back onto
human forward impulse
          with rough edges,
curling cues.
      Compressed by recurrence,
another copper, dated below what
Lincoln.

      . . . edible pith available
after great work
     so starved, to complete
the metaphor, by the love of learning.

        *

                    He knew age
as ground
for his coherent son's day
                            passes
monstrous language
                    to common usage.

                    ⋆

a reindeer's branching antlers
      gold bract

A word
a word spoken
         comes to be
                  a vocable
bearing a song, body between
         a strung thought.

A verb's passage
rolling toward
         gapingexpanse
categorical possibilities
a fiber twined.

            *

no one free

       Wound and return to wound
where inner
takes a stand

          *

Sort of tough, jean-jacket
wearing independence
of prime numbers

one by one,
all variables fail in their suit
at intelligibility but self
          and one

Stay and unstayed
stop and go
                    traffic
executions
                    hand
jaunt
journey
          path
          line of thought
love
          rest, movement

          *

replete with time
                        still still, yet

            ridge line
cloaks
rugged
expanses
                        difficult
                        where contour
                                    tips
                                    to
                                    sheer

fulfilling counter
                        argument,
                                    evidence
of water-washed
            canyons
redundant in structure
            unique by point

                        resists recruitment
                        to status, to useful
                        metaphor
an obstacle

                        not the same overland
as release from repetition
            by song.

                        ★

against dead roses
short song commuted
by formal hearing. Lulled,
sad refrain struck
           between again

He looks out his poem's window
           sees profusion
           of what must be the growing
           season,
but inside, he must hold himself
           against the ability to enter
           the vision. And given to visions,
he must make toys of forces, self
           a black hole toward which the various,
the universe runs except the stone
that can't be passed.

                         As guest worker.
A limited stay. Nothing in my name.

Thin work gloves, palm split
           open before ten. How it is.

Maybe I heard it with a shift
           in wind.

                    *

Deborah Meadows grew up in Buffalo, NY in a working class family, attended SUNY, Buffalo, worked in factory and various manual labor, and in 1977 moved west to work in a poverty program after graduation. Deborah Meadows has lived with her lover Howard Stover near Los Angeles, California since 1986. Together they built a small house in the Piute mountains on weekends, and, separately, have worked on various peace and social justice issues. She teaches in the Liberal Studies department at California State Polytechnic University, Pomona, where she has worked as a labor organizer on education equity issues, curates the Poetry and Jazz series for her students, participated in travel exchanges with writers in the campus' Cuba program, and contributed to curriculum design in the campus' interdisciplinary program.

Her works of poetry include: *Representing Absence* (Green Integer, 2004), *Itinerant Men* (Krupskaya, 2004), *Thin Gloves* (Green Integer, 2006), and two chapbooks from Tinfish Press, *Growing Still* (2005) and *"The 60's and 70's: from The Theory of Subjectivity in Moby-Dick"* (2003).

Electronic Poetry Center author page:
http://epc.buffalo.edu/authors/meadows/

★ ★ ★

www.ingramcontent.com/pod-product-compliance
Lightning Source LLC
Chambersburg PA
CBHW031929080426
42734CB00007B/607